Steck Vaughn

Target Spelling 180

Margaret Scarborough
Mary F. Brigham
Teresa A. Miller

Rigby · Steck-Vaughn

www.HarcourtAchieve.com
1.800.531.5015

Table of Contents

Acknowledgment

Cover Illustration by Dan Clayton

ISBN 0-7398-9188-X

© 2004 Harcourt Achieve Inc.

4 5 6 7 8 059 11 10 09 08 07

Word Study Plan

1 **LOOK** at the word. _____

2 **SAY** the word. _____

3 **THINK** about each letter. _____

4 **SPELL** the word aloud. _____

5 **WRITE** the word. _____

6 **CHECK** the spelling. _____

7 **REPEAT** the steps
if you need more practice. _____

Name _____

1

Spelling Strategies

plant
play
please

cat, bat, hat

Think about the beginning sound of the word that you want to spell. Then think about a word you know that begins with the same sound.

Look for word families. The first letters of the words in a word family are different. The other letters are the same. Words in a word family rhyme.

Think about the shape of each letter in the word.

s h i p

If you are not sure how to spell a word, take a guess. Then look up the word in the dictionary.

Think about how a word is spelled and then write it. Try different spellings. Look at each spelling to see if it looks right.

skatee
skate ✓
skat

doc•tor

Words with *a*

a	an	can
as	at	away

A **Circle the spelling word. Then write it on the line.**

1. (Can) you come to see me? _____can_____

2. Don't go away. _____

3. I run as fast as you. _____

4. I ate an apple. _____

5. We are at home. _____

6. He is a boy. _____

B **Circle the word that is the same as the top one.**

as	can	an	at	away
at	con	as	an	avay
an	nac	an	as	awag
(as)	cah	na	at	aawy
sa	can	at	ta	away

C **Find the missing letters. Then write the word.**

1. __a__ t _____

2. ____ a n _____

3. a ____ ____ y _____

Name _____

Lesson 1

DAY 2

Words with *a*

a	an	can
as	at	away

A Fill in the boxes with the correct spelling words.

1. | a | n |

2. | | |

3. (boxes)

4. | |

5. | | | |

6. | | |

B Fill in each blank with the correct spelling word.

1. I ___**can**___ hit the ball.
   <small>an   can</small>

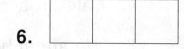

2. Are you _____ your house?
   <small>as   at</small>

3. May I have _____ apple?
   <small>at   an</small>

4. Please go _____!
   <small>can   away</small>

5. He is _____ boy.
   <small>as   a</small>

6. I am _____ tall as my mom.
   <small>as   a</small>

4

Lesson 1

DAY 3

Words with *a*

a	an	can
as	at	away

A Find the hidden spelling words.

```
c  n  f  a  s  l  u  v
m  d  o  x  a  w  n  t
l  z  w  o  w  c  a  r
a  t  i  v  a  n  p  s
x  m  d  e  y  c  a  n
```

B Fill in each blank with a spelling word.

1. You __can__ go home now.

2. Take me _____ from here!

3. She is _____ nice as her brother.

C Use the correct spelling words to complete the story.

My little brother found _____ cat. He wanted to keep it. I thought he might have to give it _____. I told my brother we could keep the cat if everyone liked it.

Dad came home and saw the cat. He looked _____ the cat, and the cat looked back. Dad smiled and said, "The cat _____ stay!" Then he found an old blanket for the cat to sleep on.

Name _____

Words with *a*

a	an	can
as	at	away

A Put an *X* on the word that is <u>not</u> the same.

1. a	a	✗	a	a
2. an	in	an	an	an
3. can	can	can	con	can
4. as	as	as	as	aa
5. at	at	it	at	at
6. away	away	awag	away	away

B Write each spelling word three times.

1. as _____ _____ _____

2. at _____ _____ _____

3. away _____ _____ _____

4. an _____ _____ _____

5. a _____ _____ _____

6. can _____ _____ _____

C Complete each sentence.

1. <u>Can</u> you see that _____?

2. When you went <u>away</u>, _____.

Lesson 2

DAY 1

Words with -ad

bad	dad	come
mad	sad	down

A Circle the spelling word. Then write it on the line.

1. I will walk down the hill. _____

2. Are you mad at me? _____

3. This has been a bad day. _____

4. My dad plays ball with me. _____

5. Your face looks sad. _____

6. Please come over to my house. _____

B Circle the word that is the same as the top one.

mad	bad	sad	come	dad	down
dam	bed	sed	come	pad	bown
wad	bud	sad	cowe	dod	dowr
mab	bad	sod	came	dad	dawn
mad	bab	sap	ceme	pap	down

C Find the missing letters. Then write the word.

1. c _____ _____ _____   _____

2. _____ o w _____   _____

3. s _____ _____ _____   _____

Name _____

7

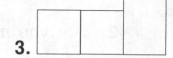

Lesson 2

Words with -ad

bad	dad	come
mad	sad	down

A Fill in the boxes with the correct spelling words.

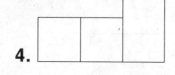

1.

2.

3.

4.

5.

6.

B Fill in each blank with the correct spelling word.

1. I am _____ because I missed the bus.
   mad   bad

2. Will you _____ home with me?
   down   come

3. I love my _____ very much.
   sad   dad

4. Go _____ the slide.
   down   come

5. My bird flew away, and I am _____.
   mad   sad

6. If it is not good, it is _____.
   bad   mad

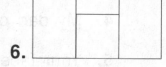

8

Lesson 2

Words with -*ad*

bad	dad	come
mad	sad	down

A Find the hidden spelling words.

```
a  b  c  d  a  d  e  f
l  m  n  o  p  q  r  s
f  a  c  o  m  e  t  a
c  d  o  w  n  b  e  d
v  y  n  x  p  b  a  d
```

B Fill in each blank with a spelling word.

1. My _____ is a good man.

2. Please _____ and see me!

3. You must go _____ the stairs.

C Use the correct spelling words to complete the story.

I have been in Florida for two weeks. I have been visiting

my friends at the beach.

Everyday we take a walk _____ the beach and

look for seashells. We are always careful to stay away from

jellyfish. A jellyfish sting can be very _____.

My _____ will pick me up at the airport tomorrow. I

can't wait for my friends to _____ see me soon.

Name _____

9

Lesson 2

DAY 4

Words with -*ad*

bad	dad	come
mad	sad	down

A Put an *X* on the word that is <u>not</u> the same.

1. mad	mad	map	mad	mad
2. bad	bad	dad	bad	bad
3. come	came	come	come	come
4. dad	dad	dap	dad	dad
5. down	down	down	domu	down
6. sad	sad	sab	sad	sad

B Write each spelling word three times.

1. down _____ _____ _____

2. dad _____ _____ _____

3. come _____ _____ _____

4. sad _____ _____ _____

5. mad _____ _____ _____

6. bad _____ _____ _____

C Complete each sentence.

1. <u>Dad</u> wants me to _____.

2. It makes me feel <u>sad</u> when _____.

Lesson 3

Words with -*ag*

bag	tag	find
rag	wag	funny

A Circle the spelling word. Then write it on the line.

1. Can you find my pencil? _____

2. A clown is funny. _____

3. Does your dog's tail wag? _____

4. I dust my desk with a rag. _____

5. My food is in that bag. _____

6. You have to tag him to win. _____

B Circle the word that is the same as the top one.

<u>rag</u>	<u>find</u>	<u>bag</u>	<u>tag</u>	<u>funny</u>	<u>wag</u>
raq	tind	bay	tar	tunny	gaw
rab	fiud	dag	rat	fnuuy	wig
rag	find	beg	gat	fenny	wag
gar	finb	bag	tag	funny	way

C Circle each spelling word that is hidden in the big word. Write the word on the line.

1. (wag)on ___wag___

2. baggy _____

3. brag _____

4. stag _____

Name _____

11

Words with -ag

bag	tag	find
rag	wag	funny

A **Find the hidden spelling words.**

```
x  b  c  w  a  g  m
n  a  p  r  s  p  o
s  g  h  f  t  a  g
s  o  c  i  r  s  t
n  f  u  n  n  y  e
b  u  m  d  r  a  g
```

B **Fill in each blank with the correct spelling word.**

1. An old cloth is a _____.
   <u>wag</u>   <u>rag</u>

2. A joke can be _____.
   <u>funny</u>   <u>find</u>

3. I pack my lunch in a _____.
   <u>tag</u>   <u>bag</u>

4. If your dog is happy, his tail will _____.
   <u>wag</u>   <u>rag</u>

5. When I hide, no one can _____ me.
   <u>find</u>   <u>funny</u>

6. I had to _____ home base.
   <u>bag</u>   <u>tag</u>

Lesson 3

DAY 3

Words with -*ag*

bag	tag	find
rag	wag	funny

A Fill in the boxes with the correct spelling words.

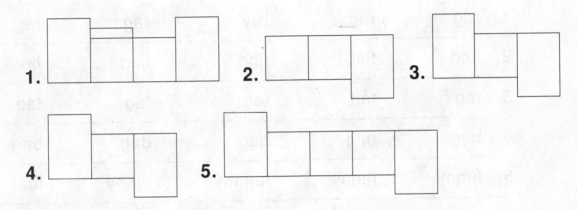

1.

2.

3.

4.

5.

B Find the missing letters. Then write the word.

1. f _____ _____ _____ y   _____

2. f _____ _____ _____   _____

C Match each picture with its word. Then write the word.

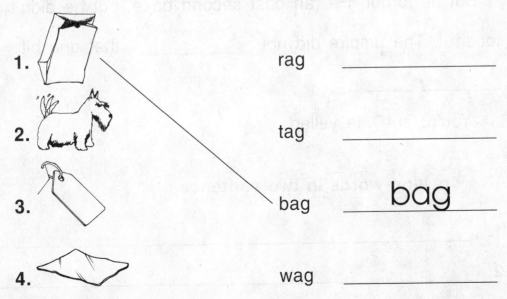

1.   rag   _____

2.   tag   _____

3.   bag   bag

4.   wag   _____

Name _____

DAY
4

Words with -ag

bag	tag	find
rag	wag	funny

A Put an *X* on the word that is <u>not</u> the same.

1. rag	rag	ray	rag	rag
2. find	finb	find	find	find
3. tag	tag	tag	tag	taq
4. bag	bag	bag	dag	bag
5. funny	funny	fummy	funny	funny
6. wag	way	wag	wag	wag

B Use the correct spelling words to complete the story.

I love to play baseball. I tried to teach my brother how to play.

"You have to _____ each base as you run," I said.

But he forgot. He ran past second base, but he didn't

touch it. The umpire did not _____ that one bit

_____.

"You're out!" he yelled.

C Use spelling words in two sentences.

1. _____

2. _____

Lesson 4 — Words with *-en*

DAY 1

pen	hen	he
ten	big	blue

A Circle the spelling word. Then write it on the line.

1. A chicken can be a hen. _____

2. I write with a pen. _____

3. You have big eyes. _____

4. The sky is blue. _____

5. He is my pal. _____

6. The number after nine is ten. _____

B Use the correct spelling words to complete the story.

Farmer Brown had _____ white pigs. He had

one white hen. He kept them all in the same wooden

_____. It was a big pen.

_____ was afraid his hen would get lost among

the pigs. So he painted her _____.

C Find the missing letters. Then write the word.

1. b _____ _____   _____

2. _____ _____ u e   _____

3. t _____ _____   _____

Name _____

15

Lesson 4

DAY
2

Words with *-en*

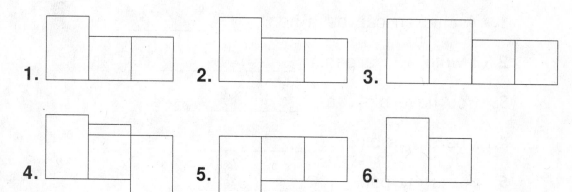

| pen | hen | he |
| ten | big | blue |

A Fill in the boxes with the correct spelling words.

1.

2.

3.

4.

5.

6.

B Circle the word that is the same as the top one.

hen	big	he	pen	blue	ten
hon	dig	hi	pan	dlue	net
heu	biy	ho	pen	blue	ten
hen	big	he	qen	bule	ton
yen	beg	hu	peu	blae	fen

C Circle each spelling word that is hidden in the big word. Write the word on the line.

1. (ten)t _____ten_____

2. penny _____

3. she _____

4. then _____

16

Lesson 4

Words with -*en*

pen	hen	he
ten	big	blue

A Fill in each blank with the correct spelling word.

1. The number after nine is _____.
   <u>ten   hen</u>

2. A chicken can be a _____.
   <u>ten   hen</u>

3. I write with a red _____.
   <u>hen   pen</u>

4. The color of her shirt is _____.
   <u>big   blue</u>

5. _____ wears a hat.
   <u>He   Hen</u>

6. One dog is small, and the other is _____.
   <u>blue   big</u>

B Match each word with its picture. Then write the word.

1. ten
      _____

2. hen
      _____

3. pen
      _____

Name _____

Lesson 4   Words with *-en*

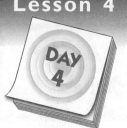
DAY 4

pen	hen	he
ten	big	blue

A Put an *X* on the word that is <u>not</u> the same.

1. he	he	be	he	he
2. big	big	big	big	dig
3. hen	hen	hen	ben	hen
4. blue	dlue	blue	blue	blue
5. ten	ten	fen	ten	ten
6. pen	pen	qen	pen	pen

B Write each spelling word three times.

1. big _____ _____ _____

2. blue _____ _____ _____

3. he _____ _____ _____

4. hen _____ _____ _____

5. pen _____ _____ _____

6. ten _____ _____ _____

C Complete each sentence.

1. I once had a <u>blue</u> _____.

2. A <u>hen</u> is _____.

Lesson 5

DAY 1

Words with -*et*

jet	pet	help
net	wet	here

A Circle the spelling word. Then write it on the line.

1. My cat is a pet. _____

2. Water will get you wet. _____

3. I need help with my work. _____

4. The fish are in the net. _____

5. Let's go in here. _____

6. Our jet plane took off fast! _____

B Circle the word that is the same as the top one.

help	jet	here	wet	pet	net
halp	get	here	met	qet	not
help	iet	hare	uet	pef	ten
helq	jet	hene	vet	pet	net
holp	qet	bere	wet	pat	vet

C Find the missing letters. Then write the word.

1. h _____ _____ p   _____

2. _____ e r _____   _____

3. w _____ _____   _____

Name _____

Lesson 5

Words with -*et*

DAY 2

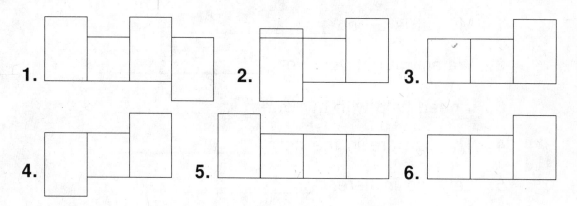

| jet | pet | help |
| net | wet | here |

A Fill in the boxes with the correct spelling words.

1.

2.

3.

4.

5.

6.

B Fill in each blank with the correct spelling word.

1. The water made me all _____ .

   net   wet

2. Ask me when you need _____ .

   help   here

3. We use a _____ to catch fish.

   jet   net

4. This cat could be your _____ .

   pet   net

   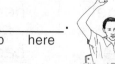

5. It's really hot in _____ .

   help   here

6. A fast plane may be a _____ .

   net   jet

Words with *-et*

jet	pet	help
net	wet	here

A Find the hidden spelling words.

```
f  i  l  p  e  t  c  n
m  s  v  c  o  m  r  e
i  n  x  h  a  w  e  t
t  a  j  e  t  c  d  r
w  i  l  r  o  c  k  s
b  a  h  e  l  p  q  z
```

B Fill in each blank with a spelling word.

1. The fast _____ got me _____ on time.

2. The man used a _____ to catch his _____.

C Match each picture with its word. Then write the word.

1.    pet   _____

2.    net   _____

3.    jet   _____

4.    wet   _____

Name _____

Words with -et

jet	pet	help
net	wet	here

A **Use the correct spelling words to complete the story.**

Dolphins are smart animals. They live in the sea. They need to stay _____ all the time. Dolphins love to swim and play. They like to jump above the water. They should not be someone's _____.

Dolphins swim near groups of tuna. Sometimes a dolphin swims into a _____ meant to catch tuna. If the dolphin gets caught, it needs _____ soon.

B **Write the spelling words in ABC order.**

1. __help__   2. __here__   3. _____

4. _____   5. _____   6. _____

C **Write each spelling word three times.**

1. pet _____ _____ _____

2. help _____ _____ _____

3. wet _____ _____ _____

4. here _____ _____ _____

5. net _____ _____ _____

a	away	come
as	bad	bag
an	mad	tag
at	dad	rag
can	sad	pen

A Match each picture with its word. Then write the word.

1.  sad _____

2.  tag _____

3.  bag _____

4.   pen _____

B Fill in each blank with the correct spelling word.

1. She will _____ home today.
   come   away

2. I dusted my desk with an old _____.
   tag   rag

3. I would like to eat _____ apple.
   as   an

4. There is someone _____ the door.
   at   an

Name _____

Review

wag	hen	net
find	big	pet
funny	he	wet
down	blue	help
ten	jet	here

C **Find the missing letters. Then write the word.**

1. _____ _____ l p   _____

2. b _____ _____ e   _____

3. _____ u _____ _____ y   _____

4. _____ o w _____   _____

5. n _____ _____   _____

6. h_____ r_____   _____

D **Use the correct spelling words to complete the story.**

I have been looking everywhere for my _____ dog.

I even looked under my bed, but I still cannot _____

him. His favorite game is hide-and-go seek. _____

tries to find a secret place in the house where no one can

find him. He doesn't hide very well, though. I can see where

he is because his little tail will _____, and he wears

a bright _____ collar. What a silly dog!

Lesson 6

DAY 1

Words with *-ack*

pack	sack	jump
rack	tack	little

A **Circle the spelling word. Then write it on the line.**

1. I have a little brother. _____

2. A bag can also be a sack. _____

3. Tack your work up on the board. _____

4. Jump up and shout! _____

5. Can I hang my coat on the rack? _____

6. He will pack his clothes for the trip. _____

B **Circle the word that is the same as the top one.**

little	pack	jump	sack	tack	rack
liffle	qack	jamp	sock	fack	nack
little	peck	jump	sach	tack	rock
lettli	gack	gump	sack	tuck	rack
littel	pack	iump	aack	tach	nock

C **Find the missing letters. Then write the word.**

1. l _____ _____ _____ l e   _____

2. _____ _____ m p   _____

3. t _____ _____ _____   _____

Name _____

25

Words with -ack

pack	sack	jump
rack	tack	little

A Fill in the boxes with the correct spelling words.

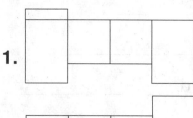

1.

2.

3.

4.

B Fill in each blank with the correct spelling word.

1. Please _____ your clothes.
   pack   rack

2. A paper bag is called a _____.
   sack   tack

3. A baby is a _____ person.
   little   jump

4. Do not _____ on my chair.
   little   jump

5. Hang your shirt on the _____.
   pack   rack

6. Ouch! I sat on a _____!
   sack   tack

Words with *-ack*

pack	sack	jump
rack	tack	little

A Use the correct spelling words to complete the story.

My _____ sister is getting ready to go to camp. She

has a lot of things to _____ for her trip. I had to get her

clothes for her since she can't reach the clothes _____

in her closet. I also reminded her to put her food in a

_____. My little sister was glad I was there to help!

B Write the spelling words in ABC order.

1. _____   2. _____   3. _____

4. _____   5. _____   6. _____

C Match each word with its picture. Then write the word.

1. tack

   _____

2. jump

   _____

3. little

   _____

4. sack

   _____

Name _____

DAY 4

Words with -*ack*

pack	sack	jump
rack	tack	little

A Put an *X* on the word that is <u>not</u> the same.

1. rack   rack   rach   rack   rack

2. jump   jump   jump   jump   jumq

3. sack   sach   sack   sack   sack

4. tack   tack   toch   tack   tack

5. little   little   little   liffle   little

6. pack   pack   pack   pack   back

B Write each spelling word three times.

1. pack _____ _____ _____

2. rack _____ _____ _____

3. jump _____ _____ _____

4. little _____ _____ _____

5. sack _____ _____ _____

6. tack _____ _____ _____

C Complete each sentence.

1. She will <u>jump</u> _____.

2. I had a <u>little</u> _____.

Words with -ick

kick	sick	look
pick	tick	make

A Circle the spelling word. Then write it on the line.

1. Look up at the sky. _____

2. Too much candy made me sick. _____

3. Do you know how to make money? _____

4. A tick can bite a dog. _____

5. Which apples did you pick? _____

6. How far can you kick the ball? _____

B Circle the word that is the same as the top one.

make	pick	look	sick	tick	kick
nake	qick	leek	sack	fick	klick
made	pick	kool	sick	tcik	keck
make	pikc	kook	sock	tick	kick
meke	bick	look	siok	teck	hich

C Find the missing letters. Then write the word.

1. l ____ ____ k   _____

2. m a ____ ____   _____

3. t ____ ____ ____   _____

Name _____

Words with *-ick*

kick	**sick**	**look**
pick	**tick**	**make**

A Fill in the boxes with the correct spelling words.

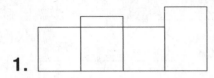

1.

2.

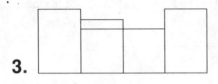

3.

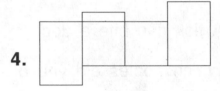

4.

B Fill in each blank with the correct spelling word.

1. I found a _____ on my dog.
   tick   kick

2. Can you _____ at this picture?
   make   look

3. Please _____ your bed.
   make   look

4. _____ the ball into the net.
   Pick   Kick

5. Which color did you _____?
   sick   pick

6. My head hurts, and I feel _____.
   sick   pick

Lesson 7

Words with *-ick*

kick	sick	look
pick	tick	make

A Use the correct spelling words to complete the story.

Have you ever seen a dog scratching its fur? It might have a _____. Ticks are little black bugs. They can get on people and pets. After you have been outside, check yourself for ticks. If you find one, don't _____ it off. Ask for help. A tick bite can make you _____.

B Write the spelling words in ABC order.

1. _____   2. _____   3. _____

4. _____   5. _____   6. _____

C Match each picture with its word. Then write the word.

 1. kick _____

 2. sick _____

 3. make _____

 4. look _____

Name _____

Lesson 7   Words with -ick

kick	sick	look
pick	tick	make

A   Write these spelling words from the last lesson.

1. pack _____
2. sack _____
3. rack _____
4. little _____
5. tack _____
6. jump _____

B   Fill in each blank with a spelling word.

1. I can _____ the ball far.
2. _____ at me run.
3. He was _____ from eating all the candy.
4. Can you _____ a paper jet?

C   Write each spelling word three times.

1. kick   _____ _____ _____
2. pick   _____ _____ _____
3. look   _____ _____ _____
4. make   _____ _____ _____
5. sick   _____ _____ _____
6. tick   _____ _____ _____

Lesson 8

Words with *-ell*

bell	tell	me
sell	well	my

A **Circle the spelling word. Then write it on the line.**

1. Can you tell us a story? _____

2. The bell is going to ring. _____

3. You are my son. _____

4. I tossed a coin in the well. _____

5. Did you sell your bike? _____

6. She gave me a book. _____

B **Circle the word that is the same as the top one.**

well	bell	tell	me	my	sell
well	dell	fell	me	ym	soll
wall	ball	tell	mo	mg	sall
woll	bell	llet	em	my	sell
will	pell	tall	ma	ny	lles

C **Find the missing letters. Then write the word.**

1. _____ y   _____

2. b _____ _____ _____   _____

3. w _____ _____ _____   _____

Name _____

33

Lesson 8   **Words with -*ell***

DAY 2

bell	tell	me
sell	well	my

A Fill in the boxes with the correct spelling words.

1.

2.

3.

4.

5.

6.

B Fill in each blank with the correct spelling word.

1. Do you like _____?
               me   my

2. _____ me how to do it.
    Bell   Tell

3. I do not feel _____.
            well   sell

4. We are going to _____ our car.
              well   sell

5. The _____ is going to ring.
      bell   tell

6. Do you have _____ pencil?
        me   my

34

Words with *-ell*

bell	tell	me
sell	well	my

A Use the correct spelling words to complete the story.

I can't wait for the school _____ to ring today.

After school I am going to visit _____ grandfather. I

really like to spend time with him. He can _____ the

funniest stories I have ever heard. My grandfather also reads

books with _____. Sometimes we even go to the movies.

B Circle each spelling word that is hidden in the big word. Write the word on the line.

1. belly _____   2. meet _____

3. teller _____   4. swell _____

C Match each word with its picture. Then write the word.

1. bell

_____

2. tell
_____

3. sell
_____

4. well

_____

Name _____

Lesson 8

Words with *-ell*

bell	tell	me
sell	well	my

A Put an *X* on the word that is <u>not</u> the same.

1. sell   sell   soll   sell   sell

2. me   me   me   we   me

3. tell   fell   tell   tell   tell

4. well   well   well   well   wefl

5. my   my   mg   my   my

6. bell   bell   bell   boll   bell

B Write each spelling word three times.

1. bell   _____   _____   _____

2. sell   _____   _____   _____

3. tell   _____   _____   _____

4. well   _____   _____   _____

5. me   _____   _____   _____

6. my   _____   _____   _____

C Complete each sentence.

1. I will not <u>sell</u> _____.

2. <u>Tell</u> me about _____.

Lesson 9	**Words with** *-ill*		
	ill	hill	not
	fill	pill	one

DAY 1

A **Circle the spelling word. Then write it on the line.**

1. They went up the hill. _____

2. You are one of my best friends. _____

3. Do not say that! _____

4. Fill the bucket with water. _____

5. If you are ill, you are sick. _____

6. The doctor said to take a pill. _____

B **Circle the word that is the same as the top one.**

fill	ill	pill	hill	not	one
till	lil	pell	kill	ton	eon
fell	lli	pill	bill	not	neo
fill	ill	qill	hill	nat	oen
tell	ell	bill	rill	tan	one

C **Find the missing letters. Then write the word.**

1. _____ n _____   _____

2. i _____ _____   _____

3. p _____ _____ _____   _____

Name _____

37

DAY 2

Words with -*ill*

ill	hill	not
fill	pill	one

A Fill in the boxes with the correct spelling words.

1.

2.

3.

4.

5.

B Fill in each blank with the correct spelling word.

1. I can _____ the pail.
   <small>fill   hill</small>

2. You did _____ do it, so I did.
   <small>not   one</small>

3. Always take a _____ with water.
   <small>hill   pill</small>

4. We went up the _____.
   <small>fill   hill</small>

5. I have only _____ pen.
   <small>one   not</small>

6. If you are sick, you are _____.
   <small>fill   ill</small>

Lesson 9

DAY
3

Words with -*ill*

ill	hill	not
fill	pill	one

A Find the hidden spelling words.

```
r  j  f  p  g  c  l  b
v  a  i  i  r  d  m  c
s  h  l  l  n  o  t  x
t  i  l  l  e  n  p  z
a  h  i  l  l  e  g  k
j  r  d  q  n  o  w  y
```

B Circle each spelling word that is hidden in the big word. Write the word on the line.

1. hilly _____

2. knot _____

3. spill _____

4. till _____

C Write a spelling word under each picture.

1. _____ 2. _____ 3. _____

D Write these spelling words from other lessons.

1. away _____

2. down _____

3. blue _____

4. pack _____

Name _____

Lesson 9

Words with -ill

ill	hill	not
fill	pill	one

A Use the correct spelling words to complete the story.

A nest of ants is called an ant _____. The nest has lots of small rooms. Many workers and _____ queen live in an ant hill.

The workers are busy all the time. They _____ the rooms with food. They keep the nest clean. The workers also take care of the young ants. The queen does _____ work. She only has to lay the eggs.

B Write each spelling word three times.

1. ill   _____   _____   _____

2. pill   _____   _____   _____

3. hill   _____   _____   _____

4. not   _____   _____   _____

C Complete each sentence.

1. When I am ill, _____.

2. The hill was as big as _____.

3. I am not _____.

DAY 1

Words with -*ock*

rock	dock	play
sock	lock	red

A Circle the spelling word. Then write it on the line.

1. Lock the door as you leave. _____

2. Some apples are red. _____

3. I put on my sock. _____

4. I fell down on a big rock. _____

5. The boat pulled up to the dock. _____

6. Let's play that game. _____

B Circle the word that is the same as the top one.

dock	rock	play	red	lock	sock
bock	nock	qlay	der	lack	sock
dock	reck	play	rod	lock	stock
deck	rock	plya	red	luck	sack
qock	roch	blay	ned	loch	soch

C Find the missing letters. Then write the word.

1. p _____ _____ y _____

2. d _____ _____ _____ _____

3. _____ e d _____

Name _____

Words with -ock

rock	dock	play
sock	lock	red

A Fill in the boxes with the correct spelling words.

1.

2.

3.

4.

B Fill in each blank with the correct spelling word.

1. The boat pulled up to the _____.
   dock   sock

2. The door needs a _____ on it.
   rock   lock

3. I took off my shoe and _____.
   dock   sock

4. My bubble gum is as hard as a _____.
   rock   sock

5. Do you ever _____ football?
   red   play

6. A firetruck can be the color _____.
   red   play

Lesson 10

DAY 3

Words with -ock

rock	dock	play
sock	lock	red

A Find the hidden spelling words.

```
l  o  c  k  r  o  c  k
a  c  k  o  o  m  o  p
y  s  s  o  c  k  e  y
m  z  p  t  d  o  c  k
e  h  l  v  e  r  e  n
n  s  a  c  d  e  n  a
o  c  y  u  v  d  t  p
```

B Write a spelling word under each picture.

1. _____   2. _____   3. _____

C Fill in each blank with a spelling word.

1. We put a _____ on the door to keep us safe.

2. Please help me find my _____ and shoe.

3. I like to fish off the _____.

4. She picked up the heavy _____.

5. We like to _____ in the snow.

Name _____

43

Lesson 10

Words with *-ock*

rock	dock	play
sock	lock	red

A Put an *X* on the word that is not the same.

1.	lock	lock	look	lock	lock
2.	play	play	plag	play	play
3.	dock	doch	dock	dock	dock
4.	sock	sock	sock	sock	soek
5.	rock	rock	roch	rock	rock
6.	red	red	rod	red	red

B Use the correct spelling words to complete the story.

I live by a big lake. There is a _____ for boats near my house. I like to _____ there. Sometimes I jump off the dock and swim in the water.

One day I fell in the lake with my shoes on. I lost one shoe and one _____. They were both white and _____.

C Use spelling words in two sentences.

1. _____

2. _____

44

Lessons 6-10

Review

pack	little	look
rack	kick	make
sack	pick	bell
tack	sick	me
jump	tick	my

A Match each word with its picture. Then write the word.

1. kick _____

2. sick _____

3. little _____

4. tack _____

B Fill in each blank with the correct spelling word.

1. Ring the _____ if you need me.
   bell   me

2. Will you _____ me a cake?
   make   tack

3. Please hang your clothes on the _____.
   rack   pack

4. I can _____ over that puddle.
   little   jump

Name _____

45

well	hill	sock
sell	pill	dock
tell	not	lock
ill	one	play
fill	rock	red

C **Find the missing letters. Then write the word.**

1. s _____ _____ k   _____

2. h _____ _____ l   _____

3. _____ n _____   _____

4. _____ l _____ y   _____

5. l _____ _____ k   _____

6. s _____ _____ l   _____

D **Use the correct spelling words to complete the story.**

Last Saturday my friend and I went to the lake to visit my

uncle. He invited us to take a ride in his boat. He has a blue

and _____ striped boat. It's very fast! Before we

could take the boat out, we had to _____ it with gas.

Then we water-skied for several hours. When my friend

water-skied, I could _____ that he had practiced a

lot. He was very good. I hope that someday I can water-ski

as _____ as my friend.

Lesson 11

DAY 1

Words with -ess

mess	came	said
less	run	see

A Circle the spelling word. Then write it on the line.

1. I can see things that are far away. _____

2. We came home after school. _____

3. What a mess you made on the table! _____

4. Don't run in the hall at school. _____

5. Did you hear what I said? _____

6. Five is less than six. _____

B Circle the word that is the same as the top one.

mess	said	run	came	less	see
ness	saib	nur	come	lass	ese
wess	said	rnu	coma	less	sse
mess	siad	run	cawe	lses	see
mees	ssid	nun	came	leas	ees

C Find the missing letters. Then write the word.

1. s _____ _____ _____   _____

2. m _____ _____ _____   _____

3. _____ e e   _____

Name _____

Words with -ess

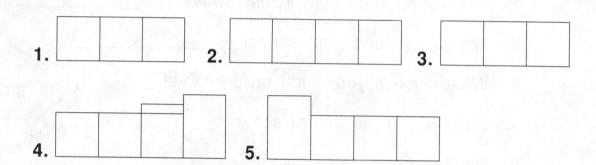

mess	came	said
less	run	see

A Fill in the boxes with the correct spelling words.

1. ▢▢▢   2. ▢▢▢▢   3. ▢▢▢

4. ▢▢▢▢   5. ▢▢▢▢

B Fill in each blank with the correct spelling word.

1. I can _____ and jump.
   <small>run   less</small>

2. This glass has _____ water than that one.
   <small>run   less</small>

3. I did not hear what you _____.
   <small>said   see</small>

4. The girl _____ to play.
   <small>came   mess</small>

5. I dropped my milk and made a _____.
   <small>mess   less</small>

6. You _____ with your eyes.
   <small>run   see</small>

Words with -*ess*

mess	came	said
less	run	see

A Use the correct spelling words to complete the story.

My friend plays softball for the Jays. They were playing a

big game against the Bears. The Bears could not _____

or hit as well as the Jays. I could _____ that the

Bears trained _____ than the Jays. After the Jays

won, my friend _____, "I'm glad you _____."

B Circle each spelling word that is hidden in the big word.
Write the word on the line.

1. messy _____
2. seed _____
3. runt _____
4. lesson _____

C Match each word with its picture. Then write the word.

1. run

2. less

3. mess

4. said

Name _____

Words with -*ess*

DAY
4

mess	came	said
less	run	see

A Write these spelling words from other lessons.

1. pill _____   2. one _____

3. red _____   4. dock _____

5. lock _____   6. rock _____

B Fill in each blank with a spelling word.

1. Three is _____ than four.

2. The house is a _____.

3. Did you _____ my work?

4. She _____ to see me.

C Write each spelling word three times.

1. run _____ _____ _____

2. came _____ _____ _____

3. less _____ _____ _____

4. mess _____ _____ _____

5. see _____ _____ _____

6. said _____ _____ _____

Lesson 12

Words with -*amp*

camp	lamp	you
damp	ramp	we

A Circle the spelling word. Then write it on the line.

1. When a mop is damp, it is wet. _____

2. Push the cart up the ramp. _____

3. You are a good friend. _____

4. I went away to a camp. _____

5. A lamp gives off light. _____

6. We all want to eat lunch. _____

B Circle the word that is the same as the top one.

<u>ramp</u>	<u>lamp</u>	<u>we</u>	<u>camp</u>	<u>you</u>	<u>damp</u>
namp	lump	we	capm	yon	pamd
rump	lomp	me	comp	yuo	domp
ramp	plam	ve	cump	you	demp
ramq	lamp	wo	camp	yeu	damp

C Find the missing letters. Then write the word.

1. c _____ _____ _____   _____

2. _____ o _____   _____

3. l _____ _____ _____   _____

Name _____

51

Lesson 12

DAY 2

Words with -*amp*

camp	lamp	you
damp	ramp	we

A Fill in the boxes with the correct spelling words.

1. ☐☐

2. ☐☐☐☐

3. ☐☐☐☐

4. ☐☐☐☐

5. ☐☐☐☐

B Fill in each blank with the correct spelling word.

1. I thought the rag was dry, but it's still _____.
   damp   camp

2. Push the cart up the _____.
   lamp   ramp

3. Do _____ like TV?
   you   ramp

4. The _____ will not turn on.
   ramp   lamp

5. We set up a tent at _____.
   camp   damp

6. _____ will have soup for lunch.
   We   Lamp

52

Words with -*amp*

camp	lamp	you
damp	ramp	we

A Find the hidden spelling words.

```
e  l  m  r  u  v  c  d
s  a  w  e  c  a  d  c
t  m  y  s  i  n  a  a
w  p  o  t  u  m  m  m
b  f  u  r  a  m  p  p
```

B Write the spelling words in ABC order.

1. _____   2. _____   3. _____

4. _____   5. _____   6. _____

C Use the correct spelling words to complete the story.

Last summer my friends and I stayed at a _____ near a lake. _____ learned how to do many things. One day we wanted to row across the lake. But first we had to push the boat down a _____ to get it in the water. Rowing is hard work, but it is a lot of fun!

At night we would sit around a big campfire and tell stories. When we walked back to our tents, one of us always carried a _____ so that we could see.

Name _____

Lesson 12

Words with -*amp*

camp	lamp	you
damp	ramp	we

A Match each picture with its word. Then write the word.

1.    damp   _____

2.   lamp   _____

3.    camp   _____

4.    ramp   _____

B Write each spelling word three times.

1. you   _____   _____   _____

2. ramp   _____   _____   _____

3. lamp   _____   _____   _____

4. we   _____   _____   _____

5. camp   _____   _____   _____

6. damp   _____   _____   _____

C Complete each sentence.

1. At <u>camp</u>, we _____.

2. My clothes got <u>damp</u> when _____.

54

Lesson 13

Words with -*ump*

bump	pump	three
lump	dump	two

A Circle the spelling word. Then write it on the line.

1. One and one is **two**. _____

2. I fell down and got a **bump** on my head. _____

3. Do not **dump** that mess here! _____

4. I need an air **pump** for my bike tires. _____

5. I have **three** books. _____

6. There is a **lump** in my bed. _____

B Circle the word that is the same as the top one.

pump	three	two	dump	lump	bump
dump	three	tow	bump	dump	lump
pumq	there	two	pump	pump	pump
pump	theer	wot	dumq	plum	bump
qump	trhee	owt	dump	lump	dump

C Find the missing letters. Then write the word.

1. t h ____ ____ ____   _____

2. p u ____ ____   _____

3. l ____ m ____   _____

Name _____

55

Lesson 13

Words with -ump

bump	pump	three
lump	dump	two

A Fill in the boxes with the correct spelling words.

1. ☐☐☐☐☐

2. ☐☐☐☐☐

3. ☐☐☐☐☐

4. ☐☐☐☐☐

B Fill in each blank with the correct spelling word.

1. One from four is _____.
<u>two</u>   <u>three</u>

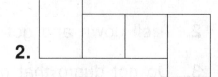

2. Do not _____ that mess here!
<u>pump</u>   <u>dump</u>

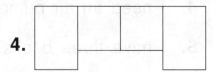

3. I need an air _____ for my bike tire.
<u>pump</u>   <u>lump</u>

4. I have a _____ on my head.
<u>bump</u>   <u>dump</u>

5. There is a _____ in my bed.
<u>lump</u>   <u>pump</u>

6. She gave me _____ cats.
<u>two</u>   <u>three</u>

56

Lesson 13

Words with -ump

bump	pump	three
lump	dump	two

A **Find the hidden spelling words.**

```
l  c  n  o  p  a  f
s  o  b  b  u  x  t
f  e  l  u  m  p  h
t  w  o  m  p  e  r
d  u  m  p  n  o  e
a  i  r  m  a  s  e
```

B **Fill in each blank with a spelling word.**

1. Please _____ some gas into the _____ truck.

2. The girl has _____ or _____ dollars left.

C **Use the correct spelling words to complete the story.**

My family likes to picnic in the park. We bring our bikes so

that we can ride on the trails. We ride at least _____

or three miles. My dad always remembers to bring the air

_____ for the bike tires.

Before we leave the park, we always _____ our

trash. My mom reminds us to watch for the bees flying around

the trash can. When bees sting, they can leave a _____.

Name _____

57

Lesson 13

Words with -*ump*

bump	pump	three
lump	dump	two

A Match each word with its picture. Then write the word.

1. bump   _____

2. lump   _____

3. dump   _____

4. pump   _____

5. three   _____

B Write each spelling word three times.

1. bump   _____   _____   _____

2. lump   _____   _____   _____

3. dump   _____   _____   _____

4. pump   _____   _____   _____

5. three   _____   _____   _____

6. two   _____   _____   _____

58

band	sand	for
land	hand	go

A Circle the spelling word. Then write it on the line.

1. I have a ring on my hand. _____

2. Do you play in the school band? _____

3. Will you go with me? _____

4. The plane will land soon. _____

5. Please open the door for me. _____

6. Sand is in my shoes. _____

B Circle the word that is the same as the top one.

<u>hand</u>	<u>sand</u>	<u>for</u>	<u>land</u>	<u>band</u>	<u>go</u>
band	saud	fro	land	danb	ga
hanb	sanb	tor	laud	band	ge
haud	sand	for	lanb	bend	qo
hand	sond	far	loud	baud	go

C Find the missing letters. Then write the word.

1. h _____ _____ _____   _____

2. b _____ _____ d   _____

3. f _____ _____   _____

Name _____

Words with -*and*

band	sand	for
land	hand	go

A Fill in the boxes with the correct spelling words.

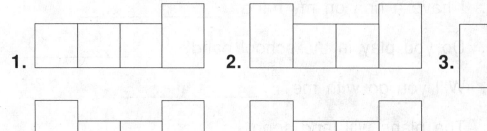

1.

2.

3.

4.

5.

B Fill in each blank with the correct spelling word.

1. Do you play in a _____?
   hand   band

2. Let's _____ to a movie.
   for   go

3. The plane is going to _____.
   sand   land

4. I cut my _____.
   hand   land

5. Get that _____ me, please.
   for   go

6. I have _____ in my shoe.
   sand   band

Words with *-and*

band	sand	for
land	hand	go

A Find the hidden spelling words.

```
f  g  h  a  n  d  s  r
o  o  l  x  h  a  a  c
r  e  a  y  b  a  n  d
e  c  n  o  v  m  d  r
k  u  d  a  n  d  i  e
```

B Write the spelling words in ABC order.

1. _____   2. _____   3. _____

4. _____   5. _____   6. _____

C Use the correct spelling words to complete the story.

My friend loves to play volleyball at the beach. He says the

_____ is very soft to play on. His big game was

today, and he asked me to come watch him play. I decided I

would _____.

I watched my friend jump up _____ the ball. He

missed it and fell on the ground. He hurt his _____.

This was not good since he plays drums in a _____.

I hope he gets better soon.

Name _____

Words with -*and*

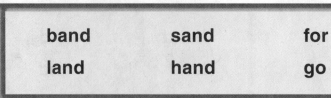

band	sand	for
land	hand	go

A Fill in each blank with a spelling word.

1. She plays the drums in the school _____.

2. We built a castle in the _____.

3. If you know the answer, hold up your _____.

4. Our house is on rocky _____.

B Write a spelling word under each picture.

1. _____   2. _____   3. _____

C Write each spelling word three times.

1. band _____ _____ _____

2. sand _____ _____ _____

3. hand _____ _____ _____

4. land _____ _____ _____

5. for _____ _____ _____

6. go _____ _____ _____

Words with -end

mend	send	where
bend	lend	yellow

A Circle the spelling word. Then write it on the line.

1. Please send me a letter soon. _____

2. Where is the cat? _____

3. She will lend me the book. _____

4. The sun is yellow. _____

5. I will mend my sock. _____

6. Don't bend it too far. _____

B Circle the word that is the same as the top one.

where	send	bend	yellow	mend	lend
were	seud	denb	yellov	nemd	lend
where	senb	bned	yellom	mand	lenb
wheer	sned	beud	yellow	mend	leub
wehre	send	bend	yellew	menb	lenp

C Match each word with its picture. Then write the word.

1. bend _____

2. mend _____

Name _____

Words with *-end*

mend	send	where
bend	lend	where yellow

A Fill in the boxes with the correct spelling words.

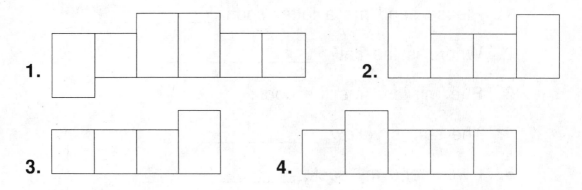

1.

2.

3.

4.

B Fill in each blank with the correct spelling word.

1. Please _____ me a letter soon.
   send   mend

2. Will you _____ me some money?
   bend   lend

3. The sun is _____.
   where   yellow

4. I will _____ my sock.
   mend   bend

5. _____ did she go?
   Where   Yellow

6. You should be able to _____ your elbow.
   bend   yellow

Lesson 15   Words with *-end*

DAY 3

mend	send	where
bend	lend	yellow

A Find the hidden spelling words.

```
s  v  t  w  h  s  t  o
e  a  x  h  e  r  e  s
n  c  y  e  l  l  o  w
d  e  o  r  b  e  n  d
e  g  m  e  a  n  e  y
r  i  m  e  n  d  b  r
```

B Find the missing letters. Then write the word.

1. y _____ _____ _____ o w   _____

2. s _____ n _____   _____

3. m _____ _____ _____   _____

C Write the spelling words in ABC order.

1. _____   2. _____   3. _____

4. _____   5. _____   6. _____

D Complete each sentence.

1. Do not bend _____.

2. Where is _____?

Name _____

65

Words with -*end*

mend	send	where
bend	lend	yellow

A Write these spelling words from other lessons.

1. rock _____

2. mess _____

3. lamp _____

4. pump _____

B Use the correct spelling words to complete the story.

My friend is sick. Her back hurts, and she is not able to

_____ over. I want to _____ some flowers to

her, but I only have one dollar. Can you _____ me

some money?

Thank you for the money. I think I will send her some

_____ roses. She will know that I care about her.

C Write each spelling word three times.

1. mend _____ _____ _____

2. bend _____ _____ _____

3. send _____ _____ _____

4. lend _____ _____ _____

5. yellow _____ _____ _____

6. where _____ _____ _____

 # Review

mess	two	we
less	damp	bump
where	lamp	lump
run	ramp	pump
for	you	dump

A Match each picture with its word. Then write the word.

1. mess _____

2. mess pump _____

3.  bump _____

4.  lamp _____

B Fill in each blank with a spelling word.

1. Please stir the _____ out of the cake batter.

2. We pushed the cart up the _____.

3. I would like for _____ to come to my party.

4. Please hang the _____ clothes up to dry.

5. I try to _____ a mile every day.

Name _____

Review

camp	sand	bend
three	hand	send
see	said	lend
band	go	came
land	mend	yellow

C **Find the missing letters. Then write the word.**

1. c _____ _____ p   _____

2. _____ e _____   _____

3. s _____ i _____   _____

4. _____ a _____ e   _____

5. l a _____ _____   _____

6. s e _____ _____   _____

D **Use the correct spelling words to complete the story.**

My cousin and I went to the beach on Saturday afternoon.

Our friend is in a _____, and she wanted us to hear

her play the drums. She can play them very well.

When we arrived at the beach, we spread out a large

_____ and green blanket on the _____.

Other friends of ours had come to the beach, too. We asked

them to join us. Then the band played for _____

hours. They put on a great show.

Words with -*ent*

dent	tent	to
sent	went	up

A Circle the spelling word. Then write it on the line.

1. We went on a boat ride. _____

2. She sent me a letter. _____

3. Are you going to school? _____

4. Let's walk up the steps. _____

5. We camp out in a tent. _____

6. There is a dent in my car. _____

B Circle the word that is the same as the top one.

went	tent	dent	sent	to	up
went	fent	bend	sont	fo	pu
want	tant	dent	seut	te	up
weut	tent	deut	senf	to	uq
wenf	tenf	denf	sent	ta	vp

C Match each word with its picture. Then write the word.

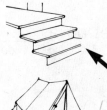

1. tent _____

2. up _____

Name _____

69

Lesson 16

DAY 2

Words with *-ent*

dent	tent	to
sent	went	up

A Fill in the boxes with the correct spelling words.

1.

2.

3.

4.

5.

6.

B Fill in each blank with the correct spelling word.

1. Let's walk _____ the steps.
   tent   up

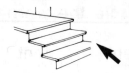

2. Are you going _____ the store?
   up   to

3. She _____ me a letter.
   sent   went

4. We _____ to her house.
   sent   went

5. Can you set up a _____?
   dent   tent

6. That's a big _____ in your car.
   dent   went

70

DAY 3

Words with -ent

dent	tent	to
sent	went	up

A Use the correct spelling words to complete the story.

When I was a child, I liked _____ camp with my

mom and dad. Dad brought the _____ to sleep in.

Mom took food for us to eat.

At the campsite, I helped Dad set _____ the tent. I

also helped cook the food. One time our cooking pot had a

_____ and a hole in it. So we had to eat cold beans

out of the can. They tasted funny.

B Find the missing letters. Then write the word.

1. w e _____ _____   _____

2. s _____ _____ _____   _____

3. t _____   _____

4. _____ p   _____

C Circle the letters that are the same in each spelling word.

dent   sent   tent

The letters that are the same in each word are _____.

Write another spelling word with the *-ent* pattern. _____

Name _____

71

Words with -*ent*

dent	tent	to
sent	went	up

A Use spelling words to complete the puzzle.

Across

3. I set up a _____.

4. My car has a _____.

Down

1. He _____ to sleep.

2. I _____ the letter.

B Write these spelling words from other lessons.

1. yellow _____   2. land _____

3. three _____   4. ramp _____

C Write each spelling word three times.

1. dent _____ _____ _____

2. sent _____ _____ _____

3. tent _____ _____ _____

4. went _____ _____ _____

5. up _____ _____ _____

6. to _____ _____ _____

DAY 1

Words with -*ast*

cast	last	all
fast	mast	am

A Circle the spelling word. Then write it on the line.

1. A sailboat has a mast. _____

2. I need all the books. _____

3. I am glad to be here. _____

4. Can you run fast? _____

5. He broke his leg and now wears a cast. _____

6. Were you first, second, third, or last? _____

B Circle the word that is the same as the top one.

last	cast	all	mast	am	fast
lost	tasc	ell	wast	am	fast
laat	cest	oll	mast	em	fasf
lasf	cost	ull	masf	an	fost
last	cast	all	most	aw	fust

C Find the missing letters. Then write the word.

1. l _____ _____ t _____

2. a _____ _____ _____

3. _____ m _____

Name _____

Words with *-ast*

cast	last	all
fast	mast	am

A Fill in the boxes with the correct spelling words.

1.

2.

3.

4.

5.

B Fill in each blank with the correct spelling word.

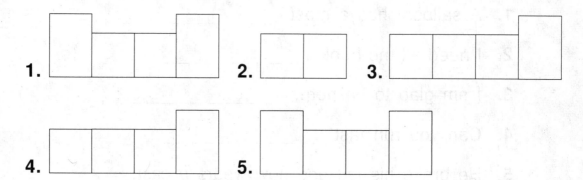

1. I broke my leg and need a _____.
   <u>fast   cast</u>

2. I can run _____.
   <u>fast   cast</u>

3. You were first, and he was _____.
   <u>last   mast</u>

4. We are _____ here.
   <u>all   am</u>

5. I _____ very happy.
   <u>all   am</u>

6. The _____ holds the sail on a boat.
   <u>last   mast</u>

DAY
3

Words with *-ast*

cast	last	all
fast	mast	am

A Use the correct spelling words to complete the story.

My friends and I race sailboats. My sailboat is very

_____. I usually win, but today I came in _____.

When I wasn't looking, my boat hit a rock. My boat was a

mess! The sail was torn and the _____ was broken.

Next time, I _____ going to watch for rocks.

B Fill in each blank with a spelling word.

1. Run _____, and you will not be _____!

2. I _____ glad that my leg does not need a _____.

C Match each sentence with its picture. Write the spelling word.

1. This is a cast.   _____

2. It is fast.   _____

3. This is last.   _____

4. This is a mast.   _____

Name _____

Words with -*ast*

cast	last	all
fast	mast	am

A Write the spelling word that rhymes with the underlined word *and* makes sense.

1. The ship lost its <u>mast</u>,

   so it could not sail very _____.

2. The turtle was not <u>fast</u>,

   so he finished _____.

B Write these spelling words from other lessons.

1. down _____   2. funny _____

3. jump _____   4. fill _____

5. you _____   6. tent _____

C Write each spelling word three times.

1. cast _____ _____ _____

2. fast _____ _____ _____

3. last _____ _____ _____

4. mast _____ _____ _____

5. all _____ _____ _____

6. am _____ _____ _____

Words with *-est*

best	**test**	**are**
nest	**west**	**be**

A Circle the spelling word. Then write it on the line.

1. Are you my friend? _____

2. The bird built a nest. _____

3. Will you be home by five o'clock? _____

4. The wind came from the west. _____

5. She is my best friend. _____

6. Did you pass the test? _____

B Circle the word that is the same as the top one.

west	best	test	nest	are	be
mest	dest	tesf	nost	are	ba
wesf	bost	test	nast	ane	be
wost	bast	tast	nest	ore	de
west	best	tasf	nesf	one	pe

C Find the missing letters. Then write the word.

1. a _____ _____   _____

2. t e _____ _____   _____

3. n e s _____   _____

Name _____

DAY 2

Words with *-est*

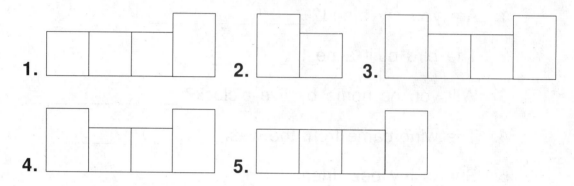

best	test	are
nest	west	be

A Fill in the boxes with the correct spelling words.

1.

2.

3.

4.

5.

B Fill in each blank with the correct spelling word.

1. The bird built a _____.
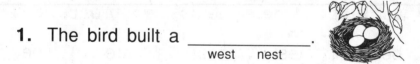
   west   nest

2. Will you _____ my valentine?
   are   be

3. Did you pass the _____?
   best   test

4. The sun sets in the _____.
   west   nest

5. They _____ riding their bikes.
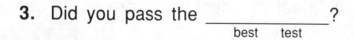
   are   be

6. My dog is my _____ pal.

   best   test

Lesson 18

DAY 3

Words with *-est*

best	test	are
nest	west	be

A Find the hidden spelling words.

```
e  l  e  t  e  s  t
s  o  b  u  n  g  s
a  r  e  b  e  s  t
s  e  w  e  s  t  u
f  r  o  n  t  s  r
```

B Fill in each blank with a spelling word.

1. I will _____ glad to take the _____ .

2. We will go _____ this summer.

3. You are my _____ friend.

C Match each sentence with its picture. Write the spelling word.

1. I get this if I am best.   _____

2. This is a test.   _____

3. This is a nest.   _____

4. This is west.   _____

Name _____

Lesson 18

Words with -est

best	test	are
nest	west	be

A Write the spelling word that rhymes with the underlined word **and** makes sense.

1. I did my <u>best</u>

   and passed the _____.

2. The bird flew <u>west</u>

   to find its _____.

B Write each spelling word three times.

1. best _____ _____ _____

2. nest _____ _____ _____

3. test _____ _____ _____

4. west _____ _____ _____

5. are _____ _____ _____

C Use spelling words to complete the poem.

Baby birds cannot _____ free

Until they pass a _____;

They have to learn to flap their wings

And fly out of their _____.

Lesson 19

DAY 1

Words with *-ist* and *-ust*

fist	mist	must
list	dust	rust

A **Circle the spelling word. Then write it on the line.**

1. I took the list to the grocery store. _____

2. There is mist in fog. _____

3. I must go home now. _____

4. There is rust in the pipes. _____

5. Dust blew in my face. _____

6. He made a fist with his hand. _____

B **Circle the word that is the same as the top one.**

mist	dust	fist	list	must	rust
wist	dust	fisf	lisf	mast	nust
mist	dusf	fist	list	wust	rnst
misf	bust	tist	tisl	must	rust
msit	bast	first	lost	musf	rusf

C **Find the missing letters. Then write the word.**

1. r _____ s t _____

2. f i _____ _____ _____

3. d u _____ _____ _____

Name _____

Words with *-ist* and *-ust*

fist	mist	must
list	dust	rust

A Fill in the boxes with the correct spelling words.

1.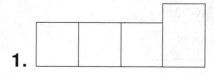

2.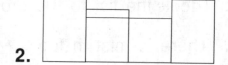

3.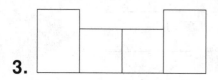

4.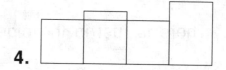

B Fill in each blank with the correct spelling word.

1. I have a _____ of things to do.
   fist   list

2. There is _____ on my bike.
   rust   must

3. I _____ have an apple to eat!
   rust   must

4. I closed my hand to make a _____.
   fist   list

5. Spray the plant with _____.
   mist   dust

6. I need to _____ my room to get it clean.
   mist   dust

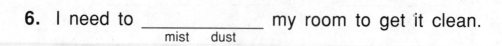

82

Lesson 19 — Words with *-ist* and *-ust*

fist	mist	must
list	dust	rust

A Fill in each blank with a spelling word.

1. It is good to make a _____ of things you _____ do.

2. Please _____ your room.

B Use the correct spelling words to complete the story.

One day I was walking in the rain. I saw an old house.

"This house _____ be empty," I thought. I looked

in a window. Everything was covered with _____.

Then I looked in the garage. There was an old car inside. It

was spotted with _____.

C Match each sentence with its picture. Write the spelling word.

1. I have a list.   _____

2. I use this to dust.   _____

3. This is a fist.   _____

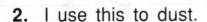

4. This is mist.   _____

Name _____

Words with *-ist* and *-ust*

fist	mist	must
list	dust	rust

A Fill in each blank with a spelling word.

1. She squeezed her hand and made a _____.

2. He made a _____ of things to buy.

3. A light rain is called a _____.

4. We _____ eat good foods to stay strong.

5. Metal tools left in the rain will _____.

6. I use a rag to get rid of _____.

B Write these spelling words from other lessons.

1. bump _____   2. sand _____

3. yellow _____   4. went _____

C Write each spelling word three times.

1. fist _____ _____ _____

2. list _____ _____ _____

3. mist _____ _____ _____

4. dust _____ _____ _____

5. must _____ _____ _____

6. rust _____ _____ _____

Lesson 20   Words with *-ter*

DAY
1

batter	bitter	ate
better	butter	but

A Circle the spelling word. Then write it on the line.

1. I ate all my food. _____

2. Do you feel better now? _____

3. Put some butter on your bread. _____

4. I want to go, but I can't. _____

5. The tea tastes bitter. _____

6. Are you the next batter in the game? _____

B Circle the word that is the same as the top one.

butter	ate	batter	better	but	bitter
bntter	afe	baffer	batter	tub	bitter
butter	ate	botter	better	bat	biffer
butten	eat	better	beffer	but	butter
buffer	aet	batter	betten	bnt	bitten

C Find the missing letters. Then write the word.

1. a _____ e   _____

2. b a t t _____ _____   _____

3. _____ e _____ _____ e r _____

Name _____

85

Lesson 20

Words with -ter

batter	bitter	ate
better	butter	but

A Fill in the boxes with the correct spelling words.

1.

2.

3.

4.

B Fill in each blank with the correct spelling word.

1. I feel much _____.
   butter   better

2. A cake is made from _____.
   batter   bitter

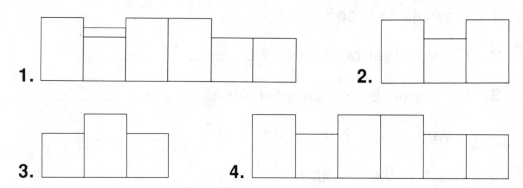

3. I put _____ on my roll.
   butter   better

4. I _____ a big apple.
   ate   but

5. Lemons can taste _____.
   better   bitter

6. I want to go fishing, _____ I can't.
   ate   but

Words with *-ter*

batter	bitter	ate
better	butter	but

A Find the hidden spelling words.

```
c a s h o u s e
a t b i t t e r
l e g o m a k e
f i s h u k o b
a b a t t e r e
b u t t e r a t
c t r e l o g t
t t a i l o v e
e e r t r e e r
```

B Use the correct spelling words to complete the story.

I made a lemon cake. But it wasn't very good. I put too

much lemon juice in the _____. It was so

_____! But I ate it anyway. Maybe next time

I will make a _____ cake.

C Write a spelling word under each picture.

1. _____   2. _____   3. _____

Name _____

87

DAY 4

Words with *-ter*

batter	bitter	ate
better	butter	but

A Use spelling words to complete the puzzle.

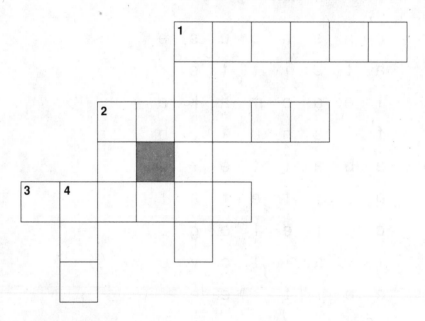

Across	**Down**
1. bread and _____	**1.** not worse
2. sour	**2.** I want to go, _____ I can't.
3. one who bats	**4.** I _____ all my food.

B Write each spelling word three times.

1. batter _____ _____ _____

2. better _____ _____ _____

3. bitter _____ _____ _____

4. butter _____ _____ _____

Review

dent	up	all
sent	cast	am
tent	fast	best
went	last	fist
to	mast	test

A Match each word with its picture. Then write the word.

1. dent _____

2. tent  _____

3. test _____

4. mast _____

B Fill in each blank with a spelling word.

1. She _____ me a letter.

2. We _____ to see a play.

3. We _____ wanted to see the same movie.

4. She can run very _____.

5. I have to wear a _____ because I broke my leg.

Name _____

Review

are	mist	better
be	dust	bitter
west	must	butter
nest	rust	ate
list	batter	but

C **Find the missing letters. Then write the word.**

1. _____ r _____   _____

2. d _____ _____ t   _____

3. _____ i _____ t _____ _____   _____

4. r _____ s _____   _____

5. n _____ _____ _____   _____

6. _____ _____ t   _____

D **Use the correct spelling words to complete the story.**

My little brother, Roy, wanted to make a birthday cake for

me. "Let me help you bake it," I told him. Roy was glad to

have the help.

We made a _____ of things we would need at the

store. When we came home from the store, we began to

make the cake. "Don't forget to put the eggs and the

_____ in the cake _____," Roy said. After

the cake was finished, we each _____ two slices.

I told Roy that his cake was the best I had ever tasted.

DAY 1

Words with -elt

belt	melt	eat
felt	on	have

A Circle the spelling word. Then write it on the line.

1. The ice is going to melt. _____

2. I left my belt at home. _____

3. He has not felt well all day. _____

4. Do you eat too fast? _____

5. Breakfast is on the table. _____

6. I have a bad cold. _____

B Circle the word that is the same as the top one.

belt	melt	felt	on	eat	have
belt	welt	felf	no	tea	hawe
balt	melf	telf	an	ate	have
belf	melt	felt	en	eat	heva
pelt	welf	fell	on	aet	yave

C Circle each spelling word that is hidden in the big word. Write the word on the line.

1. shave _____   2. gone _____

3. smelt _____   4. neat _____

Name _____

91

Words with -elt

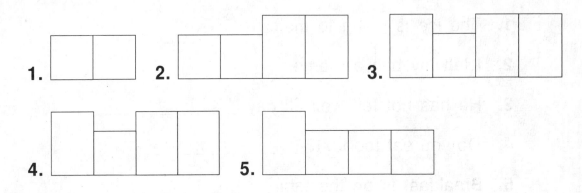

| belt | melt | eat |
| felt | on | have |

A **Fill in the boxes with the correct spelling words.**

1.

2.

3.

4.

5.

B **Fill in each blank with the correct spelling word.**

1. Did you _____ my orange?

                    eat   on

2. A _____ holds up your pants.

        melt   belt

3. I like jelly _____ my toast.

        on   have

4. The ice cream began to _____.

                        felt   melt

5. I do not _____ any homework.

        have   on

6. The cat's fur _____ soft.

        belt   felt

Lesson 21 Words with -*elt*

belt	melt	eat
felt	on	have

A Find the hidden spelling words.

```
f e l l o w m a n
e a m e f p e x l
l t a f b e l u d
t h o c e l t u g
l a b e l t o n e
e v e l k n e i v
p e a s p u s h e
```

B Find the missing letters. Then write the word.

1. e _____ _____   _____

2. m _____ l t   _____

3. b e _____ _____   _____

C Match each picture with its word. Then write the word.

1.   belt _____

2.   eat   _____

3.   felt _____

Name _____

Lesson 21

DAY 4

Words with *-elt*

belt	melt	eat
felt	on	have

A Write the spelling word that rhymes with the underlined word *and* makes sense.

1. Honey is so <u>sweet</u>

   that it's my favorite thing to _____.

2. Last summer I <u>felt</u>

   that the heat would make me _____.

B If the picture doesn't fit the word, mark it with an *X*.

belt   melt   felt

C Use the correct spelling words to complete the story.

One night I was very hungry. I went out to _____

dinner. I ate a big meal. I was so full I thought I might

_____ to take my _____ off. Maybe I

shouldn't have asked for so much ice cream _____

my pie. I hadn't _____ so full in a long time. Next

time I won't eat so much dinner!

94

Words with -lk

elk	silk	get
milk	good	into

A Circle the spelling word. Then write it on the line.

1. Candy is not good for your teeth. _____

2. Please get out of the car. _____

3. Did you drink your milk? _____

4. The hat was made of silk. _____

5. An elk is a big animal. _____

6. She jumped into the pool. _____

B Circle the word that is the same as the top one.

silk	elk	milk	good	get	into
sulk	ekl	kilm	goop	teg	into
silk	kel	milk	qood	got	toin
slik	elk	mlik	goob	get	onti
skil	ell	mkil	good	gef	itno

C Fill in each blank with a spelling word.

1. It is _____ for you to drink _____.

2. She was glad to _____ a _____ dress.

3. I saw an _____ and two deer.

Name _____

Words with -*lk*

elk	silk	get
milk	good	into

A Fill in the boxes with the correct spelling words.

1.

2.

3.

4.

B Fill in each blank with the correct spelling word.

1. An _____ is a big animal.
   elk   get

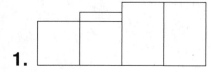

2. My dress is made of _____.
   milk   silk

3. I did not _____ any cake.
   into   get

4. I hope you have a _____ day.
   good   get

5. Come _____ the house.
   good   into

6. Drink your _____.
   silk   milk

Words with -lk

elk	silk	get
milk	good	into

A Find the missing letters. Then write the word.

1. s _____ _____ _____   _____

2. g _____ _____ d   _____

B Use the correct spelling words to complete the story.

   I was getting ready to go to a party when I heard a loud

noise. My baby brother was crying. He was very hungry. I

rocked him and gave him some _____. He started

to _____ sleepy. So I put him _____ the

crib. He fell asleep right away. I hope the baby will be

_____ for the sitter.

C Use the correct spelling words to answer these riddles.

1. You need me for strong and

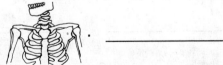 . _____

2. I am made by a , but I become fine

. _____

Name _____

Lesson 22

DAY 4

Words with -*lk*

elk	silk	get
milk	good	into

A Match each word with its picture. Then write the word.

1. silk   _____

2. elk   _____

3. milk   _____

B Write these spelling words from other lessons.

1. bitter _____   2. lock _____

3. melt _____   4. butter _____

5. sick _____   6. help _____

C Write each spelling word three times.

1. elk   _____ _____ _____

2. good   _____ _____ _____

3. milk   _____ _____ _____

4. silk   _____ _____ _____

5. get   _____ _____ _____

6. into   _____ _____ _____

DAY 1

Words with -ask

ask	mask	like
task	do	did

A Circle the spelling word. Then write it on the line.

1. Put on your new mask. _____

2. I need to do my spelling. _____

3. I did the work last night. _____

4. Ask her to come with us. _____

5. A job is called a task. _____

6. I like you a lot. _____

B Circle the word that is the same as the top one.

ask	task	mask	do	like	did
aks	fask	mask	da	like	dad
kas	kast	maks	de	kile	ded
ask	tesk	wask	do	lile	dib
sak	task	mosk	bo	liek	did

C Find the missing letters. Then write the word.

1. m _____ _____ k   _____

2. l i _____ _____   _____

3. a _____ _____   _____

Name _____

99

Words with -*ask*

ask	mask	like
task	do	did

A Match each word with its picture. Then write the word.

1. ask _____

2. task _____

3. mask _____

B Fill in the boxes with the correct spelling words.

1. **2.** **3.**

4. **5.** **6.**

C Fill in each blank with a spelling word.

1. To hide my face, I wear a _____.

2. Cleaning up my room was a _____.

Lesson 23

Words with -*ask*

ask	mask	like
task	do	did

A Fill in each blank with the correct spelling word.

1. I _____ the dishes.
   like   did

2. Did she _____ you for a peach?
   task   ask

3. I _____ to eat good food.
   task   like

4. How _____ you do?
   ask   do

5. My _____ is to do this work.
   task   ask

6. Take off the _____ so I can see
   like   mask

   your face.

B Write these spelling words from other lessons.

1. into _____   2. silk _____

3. mist _____   4. nest _____

5. are _____   6. fast _____

Name _____

Lesson 23

Words with -ask

ask	mask	like
task	do	did

A Use the correct spelling words to complete the story.

I like to _____ many things. I _____ to cook, work in the garden, and play sports.

One _____ I don't like is washing dishes. I often _____ my friend to wash them. We have made a deal. I cook, and he washes the dishes.

B Fill in each blank with a spelling word.

1. _____ she _____ you to her party?

2. I _____ not like this _____.

3. Will you wear a _____ to hide your face?

C Write each spelling word three times.

1. ask _____ _____ _____

2. task _____ _____ _____

3. mask _____ _____ _____

4. do _____ _____ _____

5. like _____ _____ _____

6. did _____ _____ _____

Lesson 24   Words with *-ten*

mitten	written	new
kitten	our	out

A   Circle the spelling word. Then write it on the line.

1. We visit our friends. _____

2. Is that car new? _____

3. Have you been out today? _____

4. A small cat is a kitten. _____

5. Put the mitten on my hand. _____

6. The work was neatly written. _____

B   Circle the word that is the same as the top one.

new	out	our	written	kitten	mitten
now	ouf	ruo	wridten	kettin	witten
wen	out	our	written	kiffen	mitter
naw	tou	oun	writtin	kitten	mitten
new	tuo	uor	writter	kitter	miffen

C   Fill in each blank with a spelling word.

1. Was the story _____ by that girl?

2. Have you been to _____ house?

3. Is that a _____ hat?

Name _____

Lesson 24

Words with -ten

mitten	written	new
kitten	our	out

A Fill in the boxes with the correct spelling words.

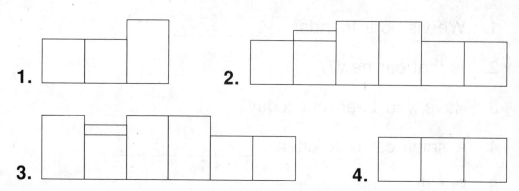

1.

2.

3.

4.

B Fill in each blank with the correct spelling word.

1. A little cat is a _____ .
   written   kitten

2. This is _____ house.
   out   our

3. I lost one _____ .
   mitten   written

4. Put the dog _____ now!
   out   new

5. It was _____ in pencil.
   written   mitten

6. Do you have a _____ car?
   out   new

Lesson 24

DAY 3

Words with *-ten*

mitten	written	new
kitten	our	out

A Find the hidden spelling words.

```
s a f l a m i n g o s
l b l o w i s i o u r
n d w r i t t e n t c
e o w e a t h a v e h
a g o a t e a r i c e
t r a i n n e w c o w
s l i c k i t t e n s
t r r e a v e s l o w
p e r s o c b m o w e
l a w o w c a r t i v
```

B Find the missing letters. Then write the word.

1. o _____ t   _____

2. n _____ _____   _____

C Use the correct spelling words to complete the story.

I came home yesterday and found a note that had

been _____ by my friend. The note said that she

had found a _____. My friend wanted me to have it.

I couldn't wait to bring the _____ kitten home.

Name _____

Words with -ten

mitten	written	new
kitten	our	out

A Match each word with its picture. Then write the word.

1. written

2. mitten _____

3. kitten _____

B Write these spelling words from the last lesson.

1. ask _____   2. mask _____

3. like _____   4. do _____

5. did _____   6. task _____

C Write each spelling word three times.

1. written _____ _____ _____

2. kitten _____ _____ _____

3. mitten _____ _____ _____

4. out _____ _____ _____

5. new _____ _____ _____

6. our _____ _____ _____

Lesson 25

DAY 1

Words with -ond

bond	pond	ran
fond	please	ride

A Circle the spelling word. Then write it on the line.

1. The duck is in the pond. _____

2. Please help me. _____

3. I am very fond of her. _____

4. We ran all the way home. _____

5. Do you want to ride my bike? _____

6. Things that stick together form a bond. _____

B Circle the word that is the same as the top one.

bond	fond	pond	please	ran	ride
band	tond	pond	qlease	ran	ride
dond	fond	dond	please	rau	ribe
bond	fonb	pand	plaese	nar	nide
bonb	foud	poud	blease	ren	edir

C Complete each sentence.

1. Please get me _____.

2. Do you ride _____?

Name _____

Lesson 25

Words with -ond

bond	pond	ran
fond	please	ride

A Fill in the boxes with the correct spelling words.

1.

2.

3.

4.

B Fill in each blank with the correct spelling word.

1. Glue will _____ things together.
   fond   bond

2. My dog _____ down the street.
   ran   ride

3. I am very _____ of my cat.
   bond   fond

4. The ducks are in the _____.
   pond   bond

5. Let's _____ in the car.
   ran   ride

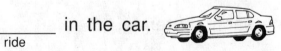

6. _____ help me find my pen.
   Pond   Please

108

Lesson 25

DAY 3

Words with -ond

bond	pond	ran
fond	please	ride

A Find the hidden spelling words.

```
s  c  a  t  f  i  s  h  a  n  d
o  n  e  t  o  n  a  e  w  o  u
c  o  b  o  n  d  g  r  a  s  s
k  p  o  n  d  p  e  a  n  e  t
b  a  t  w  o  l  o  n  g  e  t
i  s  c  a  r  e  b  o  a  t  s
s  o  n  g  r  a  s  p  l  a  t
o  n  o  t  e  s  a  e  a  t  s
d  x  r  i  d  e  t  s  t  a  b
b  c  i  d  a  r  l  u  m  e  n
```

B Find the missing letters. Then write the word.

1. p l _____ _____ _____ e   _____

2. r _____ d _____   _____

C Fill in each blank with a spelling word.

1. My dog always tries to _____ me.

2. Are you _____ of animals?

3. Let's _____ the bumper cars.

4. We can fish in the _____.

Name _____

Lesson 25

Words with -ond

bond	pond	ran
fond	please	ride

A Match each word with its picture. Then write the word.

1. pond _____

2. bond _____

3. ride _____

B Write these spelling words from the last lesson.

1. written _____   2. kitten _____

3. mitten _____   4. new _____

5. our _____   6. out _____

C Use the correct spelling words to complete the story.

If you are friends with someone, it means you have a

special _____. Many friends like the same things.

They may like to _____ bikes. Or they may like to

fish in a _____. Friends also like to _____

each other. One of my best friends gave me a surprise

party!

110

Review

belt	have	get
felt	elk	into
melt	milk	ask
on	silk	task
eat	good	mask

A Match each picture with its word. Then write the word.

1. elk _____

2. milk _____

3. mask _____

4. belt _____

B Fill in each blank with a spelling word.

1. Did you _____ all the ice cream?

2. Please _____ me, and I'll help you.

3. Can you _____ me a new pencil?

4. He went _____ the store.

5. My _____ is to mow the lawn.

Name _____

Review _____

do	written	fond
like	our	pond
did	new	please
kitten	out	ran
mitten	bond	ride

C **Find the missing letters. Then write the word.**

1. _____ _____ d _____ _____

2. p _____ _____ _____ _____

3. _____ _____ w _____

4. _____ _____ r _____

5. m _____ t _____ _____ _____ _____

6. k _____ _____ _____ _____ n _____

D **Use the correct spelling words to complete the story.**

When people are _____ of each other, they have

a special _____. Good friends often want to spend

time with each other. They may _____ to ride bikes

together or go fishing at a pond. My best friend and I like to

watch the same movies and take long walks. When people

are good friends, they try to _____ each other. My

best friend has never forgotten my birthday, and I have never

forgotten hers. We always stick together like glue.

Lesson 26 — Words with *-ap*

clap	trap	no
slap	wrap	now

A **Circle the spelling word. Then write it on the line.**

1. Please wrap this present. _____

2. I had to say no to him. _____

3. Can you clap your hands? _____

4. Come to see me now. _____

5. He set a trap for the mouse. _____

6. Do not slap at the bees. _____

B **Circle the word that is the same as the top one.**

clap	slap	trap	wrap	no	now
claq	pals	tnap	wrop	on	nom
clap	slop	traq	wrap	mo	now
calp	slap	trap	wnap	no	won

C **Use the correct spelling words to complete the story.**

The trapdoor spider is smart. Its home is a _____.
The spider waits inside. It covers its home with silk. When the
spider feels a bug walk above, it will pull the bug into its
home. Then it will _____ the bug up and eat it later.
One thing is for sure, _____ bug wants to go near a
trapdoor spider's home.

Name _____

113

Words with *-ap*

clap	trap	no
slap	wrap	now

A Fill in the boxes with the correct spelling words.

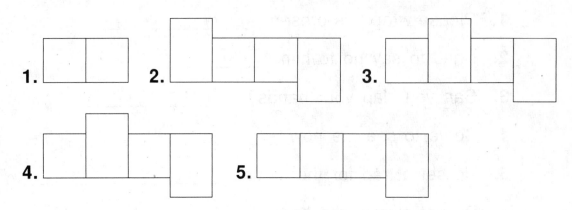

1.

2.

3.

4.

5.

B Fill in each blank with the correct spelling word.

1. Do not try to _____ away the bees.
   wrap   slap

2. You can _____ your hands.
   wrap   clap

3. Let's do our work _____.
   no   now

4. Did you _____ his gift?
   trap   wrap

5. We set a _____ for the mouse.
   trap   wrap

6. I say yes, but you say _____.
   no   now

Lesson 26

Words with *-ap*

clap	trap	no
slap	wrap	now

A Find the hidden spelling words.

```
b  i  g  f  i  s  h  f  i  n  d
o  n  o  w  a  l  a  n  d  w  a
a  o  a  r  s  a  t  e  a  r  n
t  r  a  p  x  p  l  u  m  a  d
r  i  c  h  u  p  h  a  p  p  y
a  b  c  d  e  f  g  h  i  j  k
m  a  p  c  l  a  p  u  s  h  s
p  i  g  c  o  w  h  o  r  s  e
```

B Find the missing letters. Then write the word.

1. t r _____ _____   _____

2. w _____ _____ p   _____

C Fill in each blank with a spelling word.

1. To show that we like a play, we _____.

2. To smack something with the open hand is a _____.

3. The police set a _____ for the thief.

4. I will _____ the present..

5. Do we need to leave _____?

Name _____

115

Lesson 26

Words with -*ap*

clap	trap	no
slap	wrap	now

A Match each word with its picture. Then write the word.

1. clap _____

2. wrap _____

3. trap _____

B Write these spelling words from the last lesson.

1. bond _____   2. fond _____

3. pond _____   4. please _____

5. ride _____   6. ran _____

C Write each spelling word three times.

1. clap _____ _____ _____

2. slap _____ _____ _____

3. trap _____ _____ _____

4. wrap _____ _____ _____

5. no _____ _____ _____

6. now _____ _____ _____

116

Words with *-ick*

click	flick	so
brick	slick	she

A   **Circle the spelling word. Then write it on the line.**

1. She is my sister. _____

2. My house is made of brick. _____

3. Ice can make roads slick. _____

4. Let's go so we can see the movie. _____

5. The sound a camera makes is "click." _____

6. Flick the bug off my arm, please! _____

B   **Circle the word that is the same as the top one.**

click	brick	flick	slick	she	so
clich	drick	tlick	slick	sbe	sa
click	bnick	flich	slich	she	se
cliok	brick	fliok	sliok	hes	so
klick	brich	flick	alick	seh	os

C   **Write a spelling word under each picture.**

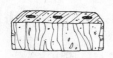 

1. _____   2. _____   3. _____

Name _____

Lesson 27

Words with *-ick*

DAY 2

click	flick	so
brick	slick	she

A Fill in the boxes with the correct spelling words.

1. 　　　　 2. 　　　　 3.

B Find the missing letters. Then write the word.

1. c l _____ _____ _____ 　　　 _____

2. _____ h e 　　　 _____

3. f _____ i _____ _____ 　　　 _____

C Use the correct spelling words to complete the story.

　　I saw a movie last night. It was _____ good! The movie was about a little girl and a dog from Kansas. A bad storm blew them to the Land of Oz. They went on a yellow _____ road. They wanted to get back to Kansas. The girl had to _____ her heels three times. When she opened her eyes, she was back home.

D Circle the letters that are the same in each spelling word.

　　　click　　　flick　　　brick　　　slick

The letters that are the same in each word are _____.

118

Words with *-ick*

click	flick	so
brick	slick	she

A Find the hidden spelling words.

```
b   r   i   c   k   s   o   m   e
g   a   f   l   i   c   k   i   t
u   s   l   i   c   k   a   n   d
e   h   o   c   e   s   t   a   r
s   e   r   k   r   a   m   e   r
t   a   e   s   t   e   e   r   s
w   r   a   c   p   b   a   n   d
```

B Fill in each blank with the correct spelling word.

1. My house is made of _____.
   click   brick

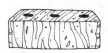

2. The ice made the road _____.
   slick   flick

3. The sound a camera makes is "_____."
   slick   click

4. _____ is a smart girl.
   Slick   She

5. Will you _____ on the light
   brick   flick

switch?

Name _____

DAY 4

Words with -ick

click	flick	so
brick	slick	she

A Use spelling words to complete the puzzle.

Across

1. She's _____ nice.

2. _____ on the light.

3. red stone used for building

Down

1. Ice makes roads _____.

4. the sound a camera makes

B Write each spelling word three times.

1. click _____ _____ _____

2. so _____ _____ _____

3. brick _____ _____ _____

4. she _____ _____ _____

5. flick _____ _____ _____

6. slick _____ _____ _____

Words with -*ing*

cling	fling	soon
bring	sting	that

A Circle the spelling word. Then write it on the line.

1. A bee can sting you. _____

2. I will be home soon. _____

3. Wet clothes cling to you. _____

4. Don't fling the bag down. _____

5. I will bring my friend. _____

6. That is a funny joke. _____

B Circle the word that is the same as the top one.

bring	sting	fling	cling	soon	that
dring	sfing	fling	cliug	sone	thaf
bring	stirg	fliny	clinq	soou	tnat
bning	sting	fliug	cling	noos	that
brinq	stinq	tling	glinc	soon	thot

C Write these spelling words from other lessons.

1. please _____   2. wrap _____

3. brick _____   4. pond _____

5. clap _____   6. flick _____

Name _____

Lesson 28   Words with *-ing*

cling	**fling**	**soon**
bring	**sting**	**that**

A Fill in each blank with the correct spelling word.

1. Bees can _____ you.
   cling   sting

2. Please _____ me my hat.
   bring   cling

3. You can _____ the ball.
   sting   fling

4. Wet clothes can _____ to you.
   cling   bring

5. I will be finished _____.
   that   soon

B Fill in the boxes with the correct spelling words.

1. 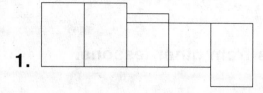   2.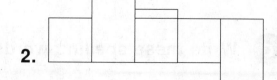

3. 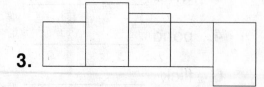   4.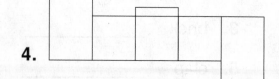

Words with -*ing*

cling	fling	soon
bring	sting	that

A Find the hidden spelling words.

```
c h o w b r i n g
l a m i c r e a m
c r e n l t h a t
h d l g i n g e r
e f l i n g l e t
s t i n g l o v e
s o o n o t w a r
```

B Fill in each blank with a spelling word.

1. I will be there _____.

2. Did you _____ your lunch?

3. Did that bee _____ your arm?

C Use spelling words to answer these riddles.

1. It sounds like fling, and _____ do it. _____

2. It means it won't be long and sounds

   like _____ . _____

Name _____

Words with *-ing*

cling	fling	soon
bring	sting	that

A Find the missing letters. Then write the word.

1. s _____ _____ n _____

2. t h _____ _____ _____

B Use the correct spelling words to complete the story.

I went on a picnic with my friends. It was my turn to

_____ flowers and drinks. I picked some red flowers

on the way to the picnic. I _____ found out that was

not smart.

There were bees in the flowers. They began to fly out and

_____ anyone who was close. All my friends began

. to run. Next time I will bring something safer. _____

was the last time I brought flowers to a party.

C Write each spelling word three times.

1. fling _____ _____ _____

2. bring _____ _____ _____

3. sting _____ _____ _____

4. cling _____ _____ _____

Lesson 29   Words with *-im*

slim	trim	this
skim	brim	they

A   Circle the spelling word. Then write it on the line.

1. I can trim the paper. _____

2. Slim can mean a small amount. _____

3. I like skim milk. _____

4. The cup is filled to its brim. _____

5. They are my friends. _____

6. Is this your pencil? _____

B   Circle the word that is the same as the top one.

slim	skim	trim	brim	this	they
slim	shim	frim	drim	that	thay
slin	shin	triw	bnim	this	thag
sliw	skin	tnim	brim	tkis	they
slem	skim	trim	briw	fhis	thoy

C   Complete each sentence.

1. Please <u>trim</u> the _____.

2. The cup's <u>brim</u> is _____.

3. <u>They</u> went to the _____.

Name _____

125

Lesson 29

Words with -*im*

slim	trim	this
skim	brim	they

A Fill in the boxes with the correct spelling words.

1.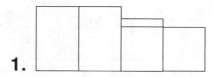

2.

3.

4.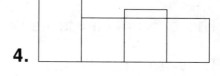

B Fill in each blank with the correct spelling word.

1. I drink _____ milk.
   <u>skim   trim</u>

2. _____ are going to the movie.
   <u>This   They</u>

3. Can you _____ my hair?
   <u>skim   trim</u>

4. Is _____ your pencil?
   <u>this   they</u>

5. The cup is filled to its _____.
   <u>slim   brim</u>

6. Running can help you stay _____.
   <u>brim   slim</u>
   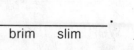

126

Lesson 29

DAY 3

Words with -im

slim	trim	this
skim	brim	they

A Find the hidden spelling words.

```
f i v e s e v e n s
c a r m y b e a n s
a o u s t h i s l i
n p a k f l o b t x
t t r i m e a r d a
a e t m e b h i s n
k c h i s l i m o d
e s e t u p p o t o
s b y t h e s n o f
```

B Find the missing letters. Then write the word.

1. t h ____ s   _____

2. s l ____ ____   _____

3. b ____ ____ m   _____

C Fill in each blank with a spelling word.

1. I have read _____ book.

2. We will _____ the tree.

3. A hat has a _____.

Name _____

Lesson 29   Words with -*im*

slim	trim	this
skim	brim	they

A   Match each word with its picture. Then write the word.

1. brim   _____

2. skim   _____

3. trim   _____

(SKIM MILK)

B   Use the correct spelling words to complete the story.

Many people care about their health. They try to stay

_____ by eating healthy foods. They _____

the fat off meat and drink _____ milk.

Getting exercise is important, too. Some people take a

walk every day. They feel that the fresh air is good for them.

C   Write each spelling word three times.

1. slim   _____   _____   _____

2. brim   _____   _____   _____

3. skim   _____   _____   _____

4. trim   _____   _____   _____

Words with -*op*

crop	prop	was
drop	stop	any

A Circle the spelling word. Then write it on the line.

1. Please don't drop the milk. _____

2. The car came to a stop. _____

3. Prop up your pillow. _____

4. I was at home all day. _____

5. Do you want any bread? _____

6. Corn is a crop that farmers grow. _____

B Circle the word that is the same as the top one.

drop	crop	any	prop	stop	was
prod	cnop	auy	grop	shop	saw
drop	enop	ang	pnop	sfop	was
brop	crop	aug	prop	stap	wos
droq	crep	any	prap	stop	mas

C Write these spelling words from the last lesson.

1. slim _____ 2. skim _____

3. trim _____ 4. brim _____

5. this _____ 6. they _____

Name _____

Words with *-op*

crop	prop	was
drop	stop	any

DAY 2

A Fill in the boxes with the correct spelling words.

1.

2.

3.

4.

B Fill in each blank with the correct spelling word.

1. He _____ very good today.
   well   was

2. Do not _____ the cake.
   any   drop

3. Could you _____ up the pillow?
   crop   prop

4. Do you want _____ water?
   was   any

5. We had a good _____ of corn.
   crop   stop

6. The car was able to _____ in time.
   drop   stop

Lesson 30

DAY 3

Words with -op

crop	prop	was
drop	stop	any

A Find the hidden spelling words.

```
p a r t y l a t e
d r o p e b p w n
a s k e s u r e e
n m a s k m o l a
y c a s t o p l t
e n e s t s t e w
o c r o p t a r s
n w a s s l o w o
```

B Find the missing letters. Then write the word.

1. w _____ _____   _____

2. p _____ o _____   _____

3. d r _____ _____   _____

C Fill in each blank with a spelling word.

1. I don't eat _____ junk food.

2. Put one _____ of this on the cut.

3. We had a big _____ of wheat.

4. She _____ on time.

Name _____

131

Words with *-op*

crop	prop	was
drop	stop	any

A Match each word with its picture. Then write the word.

1. crop

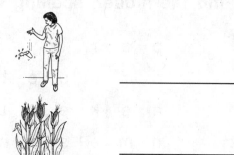

_____

2. stop

_____

3. drop

_____

B Fill in each blank with a spelling word.

1. Did you _____ your books?

2. He did not _____ at the corner.

3. Are there _____ apples in that basket?

C Use the correct spelling words to complete the story.

Jack and his mother did not have _____ money for

food. So he traded their cow for some beans. Jack's mother

was not happy with him.

But they planted the beans anyway, and the beans did not

_____ growing!

"We will have a huge _____ of beans!" cried Jack.

Then Jack's mother was very happy with him.

Lessons 26–30 **Review**

clap	now	so
slap	click	she
trap	brick	cling
wrap	flick	bring
no	slick	fling

A Match each word with its picture. Then write the word.

1. wrap _____

2. trap  _____

3. brick _____

4. click _____

B Fill in each blank with a spelling word.

1. What food will you _____ to the picnic?

2. _____ your hands if you like the play.

3. _____ is my sister.

4. Do not _____ at the bees.

5. Would you like to leave _____ or later?

Name _____

133

Review

sting	trim	drop
soon	brim	prop
that	this	stop
slim	they	was
skim	crop	any

C Find the missing letters. Then write the word.

1. c _____ _____ _____   _____

2. _____ h _____ t   _____

3. _____ h _____ s   _____

4. _____ _____ _____ n   _____

5. a _____ _____   _____

6. w _____ _____   _____

D Use the correct spelling words to complete the story.

Some people like to eat good foods and exercise often.

_____ try to stay _____ by running and walking.
This helps them to feel better and stay healthy. They also like
to eat fresh vegetables and fruits. Some even like to drink
_____ milk. They will fill their cup to the _____
with skim milk and drink every last _____. And they never
forget to drink plenty of water. They know that it is important to
drink it every day.

Words I Can Spell

Put a ✓ in the box beside each word you spell correctly on your weekly test.

Words To Review

If you miss a word on your test, write it here. Practice it until you can spell it correctly. Then check the box beside the word.

1

- ☐ a
- ☐ as
- ☐ an
- ☐ at
- ☐ can
- ☐ away

2

- ☐ bad
- ☐ mad
- ☐ dad
- ☐ sad
- ☐ come
- ☐ down

3

- ☐ bag
- ☐ rag
- ☐ tag
- ☐ wag
- ☐ find
- ☐ funny

4

- ☐ pen
- ☐ ten
- ☐ hen
- ☐ big
- ☐ he
- ☐ blue

5

- ☐ jet
- ☐ net
- ☐ pet
- ☐ wet
- ☐ help
- ☐ here

_____

_____

_____

_____

_____

_____

_____

_____

_____

_____

_____

_____

_____

Name _____

135

Words I Can Spell

Put a ✓ in the box beside each word you spell correctly on your weekly test.

Words To Review

If you miss a word on your test, write it here. Practice it until you can spell it correctly. Then check the box beside the word.

6

- ☐ pack
- ☐ tack
- ☐ rack
- ☐ jump
- ☐ sack
- ☐ little

7

- ☐ kick
- ☐ tick
- ☐ pick
- ☐ look
- ☐ sick
- ☐ make

8

- ☐ bell
- ☐ well
- ☐ sell
- ☐ me
- ☐ tell
- ☐ my

9

- ☐ ill
- ☐ pill
- ☐ fill
- ☐ not
- ☐ hill
- ☐ one

10

- ☐ rock
- ☐ lock
- ☐ sock
- ☐ play
- ☐ dock
- ☐ red

Words I Can Spell

Put a ✓ in the box beside each word you spell correctly on your weekly test.

11

☐ mess   ☐ run
☐ less   ☐ said
☐ came   ☐ see

12

☐ camp   ☐ ramp
☐ damp   ☐ you
☐ lamp   ☐ we

13

☐ bump   ☐ dump
☐ lump   ☐ three
☐ pump   ☐ two

14

☐ band   ☐ hand
☐ land   ☐ for
☐ sand   ☐ go

15

☐ mend   ☐ lend
☐ bend   ☐ where
☐ send   ☐ yellow

Words To Review

If you miss a word on your test, write it here. Practice it until you can spell it correctly. Then check the box beside the word.

_____

_____

_____

_____

_____

_____

_____

_____

_____

_____

_____

_____

_____

_____

Name _____

Words I Can Spell

Put a ✓ in the box beside each word you spell correctly on your weekly test.

═══ 16 ═══

- ☐ dent
- ☐ sent
- ☐ tent
- ☐ went
- ☐ to
- ☐ up

═══ 17 ═══

- ☐ cast
- ☐ fast
- ☐ last
- ☐ mast
- ☐ all
- ☐ am

═══ 18 ═══

- ☐ best
- ☐ nest
- ☐ test
- ☐ west
- ☐ are
- ☐ be

═══ 19 ═══

- ☐ fist
- ☐ list
- ☐ mist
- ☐ dust
- ☐ must
- ☐ rust

═══ 20 ═══

- ☐ batter
- ☐ better
- ☐ bitter
- ☐ butter
- ☐ ate
- ☐ but

Words To Review

If you miss a word on your test, write it here. Practice it until you can spell it correctly. Then check the box beside the word.

_____

_____

_____

_____

_____

_____

_____

_____

_____

_____

_____

_____

Words I Can Spell

Put a ✓ in the box beside each word you spell correctly on your weekly test.

21

- ☐ belt
- ☐ felt
- ☐ melt
- ☐ on
- ☐ eat
- ☐ have

22

- ☐ elk
- ☐ milk
- ☐ silk
- ☐ good
- ☐ get
- ☐ into

23

- ☐ ask
- ☐ task
- ☐ mask
- ☐ do
- ☐ like
- ☐ did

24

- ☐ mitten
- ☐ kitten
- ☐ written
- ☐ our
- ☐ new
- ☐ out

25

- ☐ bond
- ☐ fond
- ☐ pond
- ☐ please
- ☐ ran
- ☐ ride

Words To Review

If you miss a word on your test, write it here. Practice it until you can spell it correctly. Then check the box beside the word.

_____

_____

_____

_____

_____

_____

_____

_____

_____

_____

_____

_____

_____

_____

Name _____

My Word List

Words I Can Spell

Put a ✓ in the box beside each word you spell correctly on your weekly test.

26

☐ clap ☐ wrap
☐ slap ☐ no
☐ trap ☐ now

27

☐ click ☐ slick
☐ brick ☐ so
☐ flick ☐ she

28

☐ cling ☐ sting
☐ bring ☐ soon
☐ fling ☐ that

29

☐ slim ☐ brim
☐ skim ☐ this
☐ trim ☐ they

30

☐ crop ☐ stop
☐ drop ☐ was
☐ prop ☐ any

Words To Review

If you miss a word on your test, write it here. Practice it until you can spell it correctly. Then check the box beside the word.

Word Study Sheet

(Make a check mark after each step.)

Name _____

Words	1 Look at the Word	2 Say the Word	3 Think About Each Letter	4 Spell the Word Aloud	5 Write the Word	6 Check the Spelling	7 Repeat Steps (if needed)

Graph Your Progress

(Color or shade in the boxes.)

Number of words correctly spelled:

	6	5	4	3	2	1

Lesson 1
Lesson 2
Lesson 3
Lesson 4
Lesson 5
Lesson 6
Lesson 7
Lesson 8
Lesson 9
Lesson 10
Lesson 11
Lesson 12
Lesson 13
Lesson 14
Lesson 15
Lesson 16
Lesson 17
Lesson 18
Lesson 19
Lesson 20
Lesson 21
Lesson 22
Lesson 23
Lesson 24
Lesson 25
Lesson 26
Lesson 27
Lesson 28
Lesson 29
Lesson 30

Name